LOST NOTTINGHAM

LOST NOTTINGHAM

JOSEPH EARP

AMBERLEY

Acknowledgements

Gratitude and credit must go to the late Paul Nix of the original Nottingham Hidden History Team. I am greatly indebted to the staff of the Nottingham Local Studies Library. Thanks must go to them for their help and permission for the reproduction of certain photographs.

My gratitude goes to my parents, Frank and Lynne Earp. Finally I am indebted to my partner, Iris, for all her help and support.

First published 2025

Amberley Publishing
The Hill, Stroud
Gloucestershire, GL5 4EP

www.amberley-books.com

British Library Cataloguing in Publication Data.

A catalogue record for this book is available from the British Library.

ISBN 978 1 4456 9563 1 (print)
ISBN 978 1 4456 9564 8 (ebook)

Origination by Amberley Publishing.
Printed in the UK.

Appointed GPSR EU Representative: Easy Access System Europe Oü, 16879218
Address: Mustamäe tee 50, 10621, Tallinn, Estonia
Contact Details: gpsr.requests@easproject.com, +358 40 500 3575

Contents

Introduction

Nottingham has a long history with evidence of prehistoric activity in the area. Both Bronze Age and Iron Age artefacts have been found in the region, many by the River Trent. Despite the nearby Fosse Way situated just over 5 miles away, there was no substantial Roman presence in what is now Nottingham. Although there were some brief periods of occupation in the area, the first time that the settlement really started to establish itself was in around the ninth century. It is thought that the Saxon presence in the area represented the first substantial settlement for what is now Nottingham.

Before the sixteenth century the population probably never exceeded 3,000 people. Then it started to increase – by 1750 it was around 10,000, in the first census of 1801 it was almost 29,000, and by 1841 it was over 50,000, packed into almost the same area, that of the medieval town. Nottingham was surrounded by its open fields and could not expand to any extent until the Enclosure Award of 1865.

This overcrowding led to the appalling yards and alleys containing 6,000 back-to-back houses in the town. The government in 1844 appointed a Commission to look into the state of great towns. Thomas Hawkesley, Borough Water Engineer, testified to the Commission that he considered Nottingham to be the worst town in England. The worst areas were the Marsh; Narrow Marsh with its yards such as Lees; Knob; Byron; and Foundry and many others. In the 1920s, 1930s and after the Second World War, work was started on clearing some of these old areas of Nottingham.

Gradually the town expanded. In 1845 the Enclosure Act was passed to enclose the open fields surrounding the town. The award was made twenty years later, allowing the meadows, sand and clay fields to be used for building. In 1877 the surrounding villages were taken into the town under the Borough Extension Act and further enlargements were made this century. The wealthy moved out of the old town, mainly from the area now called the Lace Market, into the Nottingham Park and Mapperley Park areas. Nottingham became a city in 1897 by charter of Queen Victoria and was granted a Lord Mayor in 1928.

Since the Norman period (1066–1154) the layout of Nottingham and its streets remained virtually the same until the mid-twentieth century. In the 1950s, '60s and '70s, Nottingham began to see huge historic areas of the city disappear. Streets which had been around for centuries disappeared, and famous old buildings fell victim to the bulldozers.

This book sets out to explore and look at what has been lost in the city over the years. Through photographs, slides, postcards, documents and illustrations, mainly gathered from the Paul Nix Collection, the Nottingham Hidden History Team archive and the author's own photographs, we set out to examine what history Nottingham has lost to the name of progress and development.

Lost Nottingham presents a portrait of a city and a way of life that has radically changed or disappeared today showing not just the industries and buildings that have gone, people and street scenes, but also many popular places of entertainment and much more.

Buildings, Architecture and Locations

The Nottingham Exchange, Market Place, 1918. The Nottingham Exchange was erected between 1724 and 1726, replacing a shambles of buildings on the same site. It cost £2,400 and comprised a four-storey, eleven-bay frontage 123 feet (37 m) long. The architect was the mayor, Marmaduke Pennell. The corporation offices moved here from Nottingham Guild Hall. The Exchange was demolished in 1926 to make way for the current Nottingham Council House.

Royal visit to Nottingham, 24 June 1914. King George V and Queen Mary, outside the Old Exchange in the Old Market Square.

Nottingham Market Place showing the Old Exchange and the Queen Victoria statue. The statue originally stood in the Old Market Square and was moved to the memorial gardens in 1953.

Goose Fair, Market Place, 1907. The photograph was taken looking east towards The Exchange from Beastmarket Hill. For centuries, Goose Fair was held in the heart of the city on the Market Place in front of the Exchange. It gradually spread to other streets in the vicinity and, with the growth of traffic, there were complaints about congestion and disruption in the city. Eventually, the Goose Fair moved to the Forest Recreation Ground in 1928.

The Goose Fair, Nottingham Market Place, early 1900s.

Scaffolding goes up to prepare for the demolition of the Odeon cinema on Angel Row. The photograph was taken in September 2012. Built for and originally operated by the County Cinemas chain, this opened as the Ritz cinema. Local architect Albert J. Thraves was also brought in by the main architects Verity & Beverley. The Ritz cinema was fully equipped with a large stage, a Conacher 4Manual/22Rank theatre organ which was designed by organist Reginald Foort (who opened the instrument) and a large cafe/restaurant. Odeon Theatres Ltd gained a controlling interest in County Cinemas from 1935 and took full control in 1939.

Demolition of the Odeon cinema, November 2012. The Odeon closed on 26 January 2001 and stood unused until September 2012, when demolition commenced.

Selectadisc, Market Street, Nottingham, 2009. The shop closed down in the same year the photo was taken.

The Turkish Baths, Upper Parliament Street, Nottingham, 1954. The baths were built in 1898. They were bought by the corporation in 1917 and in 1950 turned into a skin clinic. The building was demolished in 1968.

Lower Parliament Street, Nottingham, *c.* 1960s. The Boots building is on the left and the Original Dog and Partridge pub on the right. Both have since been replaced with the Victoria Centre. Confusingly the Dog and Partridge pub stood opposite the current Dog and Partridge pub of the same name.

Black Boy Hotel, Long Row East, Nottingham, *c.* 1930s. The iconic structure on Long Row was designed by architect Watson Fothergill in 1887 but was controversially demolished in 1970 during city redevelopment. The first inn on the site came into existence in the seventeenth century, and by 1700 there were stagecoaches departing regularly. It was part of the Mansfield Charities set up by Samuel Brunts, and provided income for this charity. One of the earliest mentions of it is in the Record of the Borough of Nottingham for 1739–40 where Richard Shipley was recorded as having '2 incroachments by pillars &c' at the Black Boy. It was rebuilt in 1886–8 by Fothergill and in 1897–1900 he made further additions and incorporated two shops.

Plaque commemorating the Black Boy Hotel on Long Row, Nottingham. The building survived until 1970 when it was demolished to make way for a new building which was occupied by Littlewoods, and more recently Primark. Its demolition was considered by most to be 'the worst example of architectural vandalism of that era in Nottingham'.

Thurland Hall, Nottingham, 1831. Thurland Hall was located on what is now Pelham Street. It was built around the year 1458 and was the residence of Thomas Thurland. The hall was described as 'the largest and most ancient mansion in Nottingham'. It was a long, lofty and gloomy building, with massive walls, and extended backwards to within a few yards of Lincoln Street. It was principally of brick, except the end fronting Pelham Street, which was ornamented by a double row of pilasters, and window frames of heavy stonework, with an antique entrance door, approached by a flight of steps, and semi-circular zigzag pointed front to the roof. In 1831, Bailey, in his *Annals*, notes that the Old Thurland Hall and the adjacent buildings were demolished 'after having stood through several centuries, and been at one period or another the abode of Royalty, and the scene of many gorgeous and expensive festivities. Several buildings were erected, as well as the street bearing its name formed, on the site.'

Bridlesmith Gate, looking South, *c.* 1600s. This is a reconstruction based on timber-framed buildings which survived until the twentieth century. Bridlesmith Gate is unusually wide because it was one of the main routes through the town.

Rose Yard, Bridlesmith Gate, Nottingham, 1880.

Clinton Street East, Nottingham, 1962, looking northeast towards the southern end of Clinton Street East from Thurland Street. The houses are being prepared for demolition.

Bridlesmith Gate, 1946. The photograph was taken to show the problems caused by traffic congestion and obstruction caused by stationary vehicles. It was taken at the junction of St Peter's Gate and Bridlesmith Gate in the rain. Bridlesmith Gate is now pedestrianised.

Bridlesmith Gate, Nottingham, 1937, showing the premises of Sun Insurance on the left and F. E. Grain building contractors on the right at the junction with Bridlesmith Gate. F. E. Grain's sign shows the business offers plumbing, painting, joinery work, heating, fire grates and electrical work.

Clumber Street, Nottingham, *c.* 1910, looking from Lower Parliament Street.

Carrier Depot, Upper Parliament Street, Nottingham, *c.* 1890. This stretch of Upper Parliament Street lay a little to the west of Theatre Square. The tall building on the left was replaced in 1897 by the Turkish Baths. The buildings on the right were replaced by the Parliament Picture Palace which opened in March 1914. Under different names it survived until April 1957.

Trinity Walk, Nottingham, *c.* 1913. Trinity Walk was formerly called New Yard and was the birthplace of Bendigo the Boxer. The house Bendigo was born in is the house on the right with the three steps leading up to the front door. All of these buildings have now been demolished.

Trinity Square, Nottingham, 1946. All of the buildings to the right have since been demolished.

Holy Trinity Church and Hansom cab rank, Trinity Square. This image shows the Victorian Gothic Revival-style Holy Trinity Church which once stood on Trinity Square, looking from Milton Street, with Burton Street on the right. The church was built in 1841 and was formed as a parish church in 1842. The spire was removed at a later date. The church was demolished c. 1957–8 and was replaced with a car park.

Holy Trinity Church which once stood on Trinity Square, adjacent to Milton Street. This view is looking across Milton Street, over the city towards Nottingham Castle, from the clock tower of Victoria railway station. The church was demolished to make way for a car park which has since been demolished and replaced with shops and a new car park.

This image shows the commercial premises and garages of Bennetts Nottingham Ltd, automobile engineers, at 28–30 Shakespeare Street, Nottingham, in 1926. The Bennett garage fixed both cars and motorcycles.

York House was a multi-storey block which has previously been used by BBC East Midlands and Nottingham Trent University. After intu took it on it was demolished in 2014, with the company labelling it 'hazardous'.

Wesleyan Chapel, Mansfield Road – Woodborough Road junction, Nottingham, 1970. The photograph is taken looking down Mansfield Road towards Milton Street, showing the Victoria Station Hotel in the distance. The road going off to the left is Woodborough Road. The foundation stone for the chapel was laid on 22 May 1871. The church closed in July 1940 and was sold to Christian Scientists, who remained until 1951 (when they moved to Villa Road) and then the Emmanuel Full Gospel Church took possession. It was demolished in 1973.

Trinity Square, Nottingham, *c.* 1958, after the demolition of Holy Trinity Church, seen from Milton Street.

Mansfield Road, Nottingham, showing the Victoria station, *c.* early 1900s. The Nottingham Brewery can be seen in the distance. Nottingham Victoria railway station was a Great Central Railway and Great Northern Railway railway station. It was designed by the architect Albert Edward Lambert, who also designed the rebuild of the Nottingham Midland station (now known simply as Nottingham station).

Victoria railway station, Nottingham, *c.* 1960s. The station was opened by the Nottingham Joint Station Committee on 24 May 1900 and was closed on 4 September 1967 by the London Midland Region of British Railways. The station building was entirely demolished (except the clock tower), and the Victoria Centre shopping centre was built on the site, incorporating the old station clock tower into the main entrance on Milton Street (the continuation of Mansfield Road).

Victoria railway station, Nottingham – centre platforms looking north.

Victoria railway station, Nottingham, 9 May 1964.

House of Correction, St John's Street, Nottingham, *c.* 1895. The prison covered around 10,000 square yards of land and was formerly occupied as a hospital dedicated to St John the Baptist. By the time the map of 1899 was published, the building was already in disuse as a prison. It was located at the east corner of Glasshouse Street and King Edward Street.

House of Correction, St John's Street, Nottingham, *c.* 1850–90s.

Central Market , King Edward Street, Nottingham, 1970.

Shoppers wander among the stalls at the Central Market for the final time in June 1972 before it was closed and moved to the new Victoria Centre.

Hockley, Nottingham, 1984. From Belward Street looking towards Cranbrook Street Hockley Centre was a Woolworths known as 'Little Woolworths'.

F. B. Gibbs, 4 Goose Gate, Nottingham, *c.* early 1900s.

Old Town Hall, Weekday Cross, Lace Market, Nottingham, 1894. The government of both the French and English boroughs of Nottingham was carried out in the English borough. When the merchants of the town were permitted to have a Gild to regulate trade they erected a Gild Hall on Weekday Cross: this building became the court house and town hall when the borough had its own mayor and aldermen. By the eighteenth century the town's growing prosperity meant that the market place in the old French borough increased in importance and the corporation had a greater administrative workload. Consequently, in 1722 the corporation decided to build a new town hall in the market place. This building became known as the Exchange and was used for a variety of social and ceremonial purposes. The old town hall on Weekday Cross, however, continued to be used alongside the Exchange and was refaced with brick in 1744.

Old Town Hall, High Pavement, Lace Market, Nottingham, *c.* 1860–90s. The growth in municipal business in the 1870s underlined the inadequacy of the old town hall, so a new guildhall was opened in Burton Street and the old town hall was abandoned by the corporation in 1877. The Great Central Railway bought the site in 1894 for £70 and demolished the building the following year to make way for the railway line from Victoria station which emerged from a tunnel at Weekday Cross.

Ice Stadium, Nottingham, 1992. The Nottingham Ice Stadium was an ice rink in Nottingham from 1939 to 2000. It had a capacity of 2,800 for hockey games. The building was first opened in 1939 but it was quickly called upon for other purposes. When the war ended, the building soon returned to being a recreational and ice sport building. A year after the end of the war, the Ice Stadium became the home of the Nottingham Panthers ice hockey team, who would use the facility until it closed, albeit with a twenty-year break. When the Panthers disbanded in 1960, the rink continued to be used for ice skating and some other ice sports and would be where Torvill and Dean would practice in their early years.

Nottingham Panthers, Ice Stadium, Baker Gate/Lower Parliament Street, Nottingham, 2000. This photograph was taken at the final game in the Ice Stadium against Newcastle's River Kings. The Panthers were re-established in 1980 and the Ice Stadium became renowned as one of the most intimidating places for opposition ice hockey teams to visit. In 1996, plans were announced to replace the ageing building with a modern arena and a new skating pad. The Nottingham Ice Stadium was closed after sixty-one years in 2000. The building was demolished soon afterwards to allow for the completion of the National Ice Centre.

Almshouses, Barker Gate, Lace Market, Nottingham, *c.* 1750. This illustration is from Charles Deering's *Nottinghamia Vetus et Nova*, or an *Historical Account of the Ancient and present Estate of the Town of Nottingham*, published in 1751.

Warser Gate, Lace Market, 1970, showing demolition of property on the corner of Warser Gate and St Mary's Gate.

Willoughby Almshouses, Fisher Gate, Nottingham, *c.* 1910. In Fisher Gate stood the seven almshouses, which comprised the Willoughby Hospital. Less impressive than it sounds, this series of small dwelling-houses was built in 1780 when the hospital moved from Malin Hill. The almshouses were eventually pulled down in the spring of 1916.

Councillors inspecting the Old Trent Bridge prior to demolition *c.* 1869. This picture shows the old medieval bridge, and also shows the old Town Arms building which was also rebuilt at a later date. The view is looking across the river from the West Bridgford side. A bridge has existed at or around the current location since 924.

The Old Trent Bridge, Trent Bridge, Nottingham, *c.* 1860s. This picture presumably pre-dates 1872 as the bridge was demolished in this year.

Pillar with famous heads, Broadmarsh, 1996. The heads were taken off the Montague Burton shop which stood at the corner of Broadmarsh and Carrington Street. Pictured in this image are the heads of Nelson, Newton, Reynolds, Shakespeare and Robert Burns. In 2009 with 'improvements' to the area, the pillar was pulled down. The heads were stored at the council's compound on Sussex Street but were stolen and never seen again.

St Stephen's Church, Bunkers Hill, Nottingham. St Stephen's is one of Nottingham's lost Victorian churches. Built in 1859 and extended in 1868, it was demolished in 1896 to make way for the Great Central railway station (the Victoria station) in the area of Nottingham formerly known as the Charlotte Street area. Since the demolition of the station, and the building of the Victoria Centre, this area has undergone a further phase of change, and the site of St Stephen's is now lost somewhere beneath the Victoria Centre. After the church closed, artefacts were moved to a new St Stephen's church built in Hyson Green.

Chapel Bar, Nottingham, 1740. Chapel Bar was the old west gate into the walled enclosure of Nottingham and it was erected sometime around 1154 (that is early in Henry II's reign). There are, of course, no traces of it left, but there are illustrations which show it to have been just an ordinary, normal town gateway with two drum towers flanking an entrance passage which would be closed by a door possibly reinforced with a portcullis. The origin of the name Chapel Bar is obscure. Some people think that it is derived from the fact that the northern bastion of the gatehouse was used as a chapel, while there are others who are of the opinion that the whole division of the town in which it stood and which included Angel Row, St James's Street, Friar Lane and so forth was called Chapel Ward because of the mysterious St James's Chapel which stood within its bounds, and that Chapel Bar takes its name from this division of the town. The old gateway was so much in the way of traffic that in 1743 it was entirely demolished, and two years later, in 1745, when Bonnie Prince Charlie had got as near to the town as Derby, the authorities wished very heartily that they had not pulled it down.

Collin's Almshouses *c.* 1944. The almshouses were erected in 1709 on a site between Friar Lane and Hounds Gate. They were arranged around quadrangle connected by a limetree walk to a detached pair of separate lodges. Pevsner in his *Buildings of England: Nottinghamshire* described the buildings as 'a lovely group ... one of the best almshouses of its date in England'. Elaborate carved cartouches above the entrance contained descriptions of their foundations under the will of the wealthy mercer Abel Colin and their erection by his nephew Thomas Smith, the banker. The almshouses were demolished in 1956.

Jessamine Cottages, Old Workhouse Yard, Gillyflower Hill, Nottingham, *c.* early 1900s. Jessamine Cottages were formerly called Workhouse Yard. These cottages were erected in 1729 by the parish of St Nicholas to act as a workhouse, and they remained in such use until 1815. The old name for the hillock upon which these houses stand was Gillyflower or July Flower Hill, because of the wild wallflowers which grew upon it. In 1815 the workhouse was divided into tenements. Gradually they fell into disrepair and many, in the 1950s, were overgrown with rambling weeds. In the 1940s there was much discussion, and lively controversy, in the press about how this picturesque corner of Nottingham might be preserved. The premises were offered by the corporation to Nottingham Archaeological Society at a nominal rent to serve as a possible headquarters as repository of relics of bygone Nottingham, but this offer was refused because of the condition of the cottages and the cost involved in repairing them. When the time came to demolish the cottages they had been condemned for many years. Describing the cottages, a local writer said that 'Their picturesque gables, dormer windows and the patch of garden in front of them surrounded with hollyhocks, lupins and jessamine make an old-world atmosphere that never fails to enrapture visitors.' They were still in use after the Second World War and were demolished in 1956 to make way for the building of Peoples College.

Public Houses and Nightclubs

The Gate Hangs Well public house *c.* 1900.
The Gate Hangs Well was located on the corner of Brewhouse Yard and Castle Road. The pub closed in 1905. It was linked by a series of caves that were carved out of the sandstone rocks behind it.

The Gate Hangs Well public house *c.* 1900–05.
It has been suggested that the Gate Hangs Well and the Trip to Jerusalem served as breweries for the castle above, taking their water from the River Leen which ran close by (now underground). Thomas Sandby, the famous Nottingham artist, produced an illustration in 1741 which shows the area in detail, including trees, 'rock cottages', chimneys and the Gate Hangs Well public house. The Gate Hangs Well is seen here in this photograph of *c.* early 1900s in a derelict state. Shortly after this photograph was taken the pub was demolished.

Flying Horse Hotel, The Poultry, Nottingham, around 1960s. The Flying Horse inn is a former public house in Nottingham established around 1483. It stands upon the site of the house which the Plumptre family erected for themselves when they first came to Nottingham in the thirteenth century. The first information of 'The Flying Horse' is from 1400 when John de Plumtre founded Plumptre Hospital. The property forming the endowment included the oldest portion of The Flying Horse in The Poultry. In the eighteenth century it was called the 'Travellers Inn'. In 1799 'The Flying Horse' was in the possession of one William Rowbotham. The house was described as being at the Hen Cross. In 1813, a great dinner was held to celebrate victory over Napoleon. A figure of Napoleon had been brought from London by coach, and this was burned in the Market Place amidst scenes of excitement and rejoicing.

The Flying Horse Hotel, The Poultry, city centre. By 1818, the owner of The Flying Horse was Robert Mackley. In 1826 the rent was £63 a year. The building was in bad condition and scarcely habitable. After repair the rent increased to £100 a year. In 1832 Jane Clark occupied the inn. It was heavily restored in 1935. It survived as a public house until 1989, when it was converted into a shop. It is now at the entrance to the Flying Horse Walk shopping mall.

Talbot Inn on Long Row *c.* 1850. Thomas Cooper Moore's painting shows the original Talbot which was demolished. A new Talbot opened in 1876, with the facade that can be seen today. It was sold at auction in 1929 to Yates' Wine Lodge. The Talbot was established in 1380. The original Talbot Inn was used by the Talbot family when they had business in the city. This family later became the Earls of Shrewsbury.

Vernon Arms, Waverley Street, Arboretum, Nottingham. The pub closed in 2012.

Queen Elizabeth, Bottle Lane, city centre. The pub closed in 2000.

The Palais nightclub, Lower Parliament Street, Nottingham, *c.* 1970s. Nottingham's Palais de Danse opened on the corner of King Edward Street, John Street and Convent Street (now Upper Parliament Street) on 24 April 1925. The outside is distinguished by the large ornate globe above the entrance. Inside, it had colourful frescos running around the walls. The Palais could accommodate up to 1,000 dancers at any one time. In the early days, music was often broadcast on the radio from the venue.

Rotating dance floor at the Palais *c.* 1960s. The site became vacant when Nottingham Prison was demolished. The building was constructed by the Midland Palais de Danse Company and opened as a dance hall and billiard saloon under the name Palais de Danse. The architects were Alfred John Thraves and Henry Hardwick Dawson and the contractors were W. and J. Simons. The building featured a globe and frieze of dancers over the entrance. It opened to invited guests on 22 April 1925 and to the general public two days later. During the late 1980s, the Palais de Danse became the popular nightclub Ritzys. It was refurbished in around 2004.

The Old Cricket Players, Barker Gate, city centre. The pub closed in 2003.

Newcastle Arms, North Sherwood Street, city centre. The pub closed in 2009.

Old Corner Pin, Upper Parliament Street/Clumber Street junction, Nottingham, 1926. The Old Corner Pin was at the junction of Clumber Street and Upper Parliament Street and was a Home Ales public house. It closed in 1989 and has been in retail use ever since.

Another photograph showing The Old Corner Pin, Upper Parliament Street/Clumber Street junction, Nottingham. The pub was a small Home Ales tied house that was situated in a very busy area on the corner of Clumber Street and Upper Parliament Street. Once inside there was an L-shaped room that was carpeted and had comfortable seating – more like a lounge. The pub served two real ales on the bar. At one time you could only get drinks in half-pint glasses. With this pub being in the main shopping area the pressure to turn it into retail space was high, and this finally happened in the late 1990s when the pub became a Disney Store, called Disney at the Old Corner Pin. All signs of this pub have now been taken down and the building is used for retail once again.

Sir Charles Napier, North Sherwood Street, Nottingham, 1864. The Sir Charles Napier was situated at 209 North Sherwood Street.

Sir Charles Napier, North Sherwood Street, Nottingham, 1995. This pub closed *c.* 2011 and was converted to student accommodation.

Saracen's Head, North Sherwood Street, Nottingham, 1983. This pub closed in 2009 and was converted to student accommodation.

The Bee Hive Inn, Nottingham, *c.* 1920s. This pub was situated on Millstone Lane, which no longer exists. It was supposedly the first public place where John Merrick (the Elephant Man) was 'exhibited' by music hall promoter Sam Torr. Joseph Merrick wrote to Torr asking for employment as an exhibited 'freak' so that he could escape the grinding poverty of life in the workhouse. Torr visited Merrick and agreed to his request, persuading three other managers (Mr J. Ellis, George Hitchcock and 'Professor' Sam Roper) to come in with him to form a syndicate and exhibit Merrick initially around the Nottingham and Leicester area. It was Torr and Ellis who suggested that Merrick should present himself as 'the Elephant Man'.

Black Boy Hotel, Long Row East, 9 October 1969. An inn had stood on this site for many years when it was rebuilt by Watson Fothergill in 1887–88. He later extended and added to the hotel in 1897. With its massive central tower with dark wooden gables and a Bavarian balcony with a dark-wood balustrade, it was a major landmark in Nottingham city centre until its demolition in the late 1960s. It was replaced by the concrete 1960s-style Littlewoods shop.

Flying Horse hotel, Poultry, 1987. This photograph was taken during demolition before the site was redeveloped as a designer shopping arcade. It shows a general view of the demolition site.

That's Entertainment!

The (Hippodrome) Gaumont. Barrasford's Royal Palace of Varieties on the corner of Wollaton Street and Goldsmith Street, Nottingham, opened as a theatre on 28 September 1908. In 1927 it became the Royal Hippodrome cinema until 16 February 1948. It was later renamed the Gaumont. It closed on 16 January 1971 and was demolished in February 1973.

King's Theatre, Market Street, Nottingham, *c.* 1900. Built in 1875 as the Alexandra, it had a skating rink on the ground floor and a shooting gallery in the basement. Converted into a music hall called the Talbot in 1876, it changed names to the Gaiety in 1889, and again in 1901 to the King's. It became a full-time cinema, Scala, in March 1913. In April 1964 it became the News and Cartoon cinemas showing a diet of news, shorts and cartoons. In November 1967 it became the Classic and became a three-screen cinema in 1972 – screen three becoming the Tatler Film Club with fifty seats. This later became Club 2000. The whole building closed in September 1984 and was reconstructed in 1985–86 to become a medieval banquet hall. This failed and the building was demolished in 1988. The old cinema entrance is where the pedestrian entrance to the multi-storey car park is that now sits on the old site.

The Odeon cinema, Angel Row, Nottingham, *c.* 2000. The Odeon chain was set up by Oscar Deutsch in the early 1930s. The Rank Organisation under J. Arthur Rank acquired Odeon Theatres following Oscar Deutsch's sudden death in 1941. In 1960 The Rank Organisation embarked on a programme of theatre modernisation. The Angel Row cinema benefited from its development with a huge screen and 'sophisticated' foyer. The site was previously occupied by the Ritz cinema. At the new cinema, cheaper seats were in the first two rows at the front ranging to more expensive seats at the back. The venue also provided staging for pop events in the 1960s with 'Mersey Sound' bands.

The interior of the Odeon cinema, Angel Row, Nottingham.

The Odeon cinema, Angel Row, Nottingham, interior. The Beatles played at the Odeon, Nottingham, on 12 December 1963. Later the cinema was refurbished as a multi-screen cinema. On 21 February 2000, The Rank Organisation announced it was to sell the Odeon chain for £280m to Cinven, the venture capital group that owned ABC cinemas. Under the deal – which marked Rank's exit from the cinema business – the chains merged but kept the name of Odeon, the UK's biggest cinema estate at the time. Sadly, the Nottingham Odeon did not survive the takeover

Empire Theatre interior, Theatre Square, South Sherwood Street, Nottingham, 1941. The theatre was demolished in 1962.

Moulin Rouge cinema, Milton Street, *c.* 1960. This cinema opened as the Victoria Electric in 1910; the name changed to Moulin Rouge in December 1960. It closed in 1970 and was demolished for shopping development.

Parliament Picture Palace, Parliament Street, Nottingham, *c.* 1914. Opened in March 1914 with 600 seats, the main entrance was on Parliament Street, but there was a secondary entrance on Wollaton Street. After a few changes in ownership and names it became known as the News House in July 1935 until July 1956 when it was renamed the Odd Hour Cinema. It was closed in April 1957 and sold off for redevelopment following the death of the owner. As its name suggests, it ran news, shorts and cartoons for most of its lifespan. The film being advertised is *The Antique Brooch*.

Upper Parliament Street, Nottingham, 1957, showing the Elite Cinema. It opened in August 1921 as a 1,450-seat auditorium complete with restaurant, three cafes and a ballroom spread over four floors. It became the number one spot in the city, being the first to show a full-length talkie, after which it went back to silent films for another six months. Sadly it was reduced to playing 'off-circuit' material, revivals and second runs to the Carlton/ABC. It closed in April 1977.

Nottingham Royal Hippodrome, 1908. Nottingham's Royal Hippodrome Theatre opened on 28 September 1906 – the last of Thomas Barrasford's nationwide chain of variety theatres to be built. It had three circle levels above the stalls: a dress circle, circle and the upper circle (or 'the gods' as they were known), so high that only the ceiling, chandeliers and projection box were higher. The Hippodrome Theatre was taken over by the Provincial Cinematograph Theatres (PCT) chain in June 1927, and closed as a live theatre in October 1927. After refurbishment, it reopened as a cinema on 7 November 1927, with Gloria Swanson in *The Loves of Sonya* supported by the documentary *Our Prince*, about the life of the Prince of Wales. In February 1929, PCT were taken over by the Gaumont British Theatres chain. The Gaumont was closed by the Rank Organisation on 16 January 1971 with Robert Stevens in *The Private Life of Sherlock Holmes*. The cinema, like many others, was the victim of falling attendances. The Gaumont building was demolished in February 1973, and an office block named Barrasford House was built on the site. In recent years part of the building became a nightclub.

Industry and Transport

Off to the seaside. The crowded platforms at Nottingham Victoria station in July 1957, only ten years before the station was demolished.

The interior of one of the dining rooms at Nottingham Victoria station, 1902.

Broadmarsh bus station, Canal Street, Nottingham, 1978. The bus station was situated in Nottingham city centre adjacent to the Broadmarsh Shopping Centre, underneath its multi-storey car park. It was bordered by Canal Street (A6008 road) and could be accessed from the shopping centre. The station was 250 metres (270 yards) away from Nottingham railway and tram stations.

Broadmarsh bus station, Canal Street, Nottingham, 16 June 2017. This photograph was taken just prior to the bus station's closure and eventual demolition. Broadmarsh had a total of sixteen bays. Trent Barton were the main provider of bus services from the bus station, with other services provided by Centrebus, Kinchbus and University of Nottingham Hopper Bus services. Services from Broadmarsh operated mainly to villages or towns such as Bingham, Loughborough, Long Eaton and Oakham. National Express services also operated to and from Broadmarsh. Nottingham City Transport services that served the Broadmarsh Shopping Centre went from bus stands which were located on Collin Street. The bus station closed on 9 July 2017 as part of a redevelopment of the area.

Nottingham trolleybus at the King Street terminus, April 1966. The Nottingham trolleybus service opened on 10 April 1927. It gradually replaced the Nottingham tramway network. By the standards of the various now-defunct trolleybus systems in the United Kingdom, the Nottingham system was a medium-sized one, with a total of eight routes and a maximum fleet of 157 trolleybuses. It was closed on 30 June 1966. Nottingham was also served by another system, the Nottinghamshire and Derbyshire trolleybus system, which was in operation between 1932 and 1953. Six of the former Nottingham system trolleybuses are preserved. Four of them are at the Trolleybus Museum at Sandtoft, Lincolnshire, and the other two are in a private collection in Boughton, Nottinghamshire.

City Transport depot in Lower Parliament Street, Nottingham, *c.* 1930s. This photograph shows trams arrayed alongside trolleybuses.

The first electric tram in Nottingham. The first electric tram leaves from Sherwood to Nottingham's market place on 1 January 1901. The ride cost 2d. Demand for the service was so great that more trams were put on to cope, increasing the every five minutes service to every three minutes at peak times.

A large crowd gathering together for the last tram in Nottingham *c.* 1936. The 190 tram pulled into its city centre depot for the last time in 1936. The first tram routes, which were horse-pulled, opened in Nottingham on 17 September 1878. Gradually routes were replaced by trolleybuses, or motorbuses, until in 1936 only the Mapperley and Arnold routes remained. The Mapperley route changed to motorbuses on 2 February and on 6 September the same thing happened on the Arnold route, marking the end of the first generation of trams in Nottingham.

Electricity generating substation, Talbot Street, Nottingham, *c.* 1898. The electricity substation was located on the site of the later Royal Hotel and car park. By 1923 Nottingham Corporation operated three electricity generating stations: Talbot Street, with an electrical rating of 4,106 kW; Eastcroft (refuse) destructor, electrical rating 441 kW; and St Ann's, electrical rating 6,040 kW. These stations generated a total of 23.641 GWh of electricity in 1923. This was used for lighting and domestic supplies, public lighting, traction and power. The annual revenue from sales of electricity was £263,557, and the surplus of revenue in excess of expenses was £117,210. By 1920 Nottingham Corporation wished to develop its electricity supply and planned Wilford power station to use coal from the nearby Clifton mine.

Electricity generating substation, Talbot Street, Nottingham, 1901. The electricity substation was located on the site of what would later become the Royal Hotel. Pictured here are Lancashire Boilers by Edkin Danks and Co. of Oldham.

Weekday Cross Junction viaduct, Broadmarsh, 24 August 2014. This formerly carried the Great Central Railway line.

The end of the line for the viaduct, Broadmarsh, Nottingham, 24 August 2014. This photograph shows the old Weekday Cross Junction viaduct in Broadmarsh. It was taken just prior to the viaduct being demolished.

Lace workers, Stoney Street, *c.* early 1900s, looking south from Carlton Street and Goose Gate and showing the Nags Head pub. The invention of the knitting frame by William Lee of Calverton in Nottinghamshire radically changed Nottingham for ever and eventually gave the Lace Market its name. Richard Arkwright established a small cotton mill in Hockley in 1768 and this led to the development of back-to -back housing for mill workers. Lace was manufactured on a frame adapted from that of William Lee and was further improved by John Heathcote and John Levers in the early nineteenth century. By the 1840s lace making was changing from a domestic industry into an international export. This resulted in the high-density warehouses and narrow streets that are characteristic of the area today.

Hansom cab rank outside St Mary's Church, Lace Market, Nottingham, *c.* 1890.

A Beardmore taxi belonging to Jolley's Taxis Ltd, Milton Street – Victoria railway station taxi rank *c.* 1933.

London Road Low Level station, Nottingham, *c.* 1880s/90s. The station was opened in 1857 by the Great Northern Railway (GNR). It was designed by local architect Thomas Chambers Hine. GNR trains originally used the Midland station in Nottingham, but there were frequent disputes. To solve the problem, the GNR opened its own station. When Nottingham Victoria railway station was opened in 1900, the Great Northern had to construct a new chord line. The new chord line included a station on an island platform, reached by means of a staircase from the booking office on the same approach road to the earlier London Road terminus. To avoid confusion the new station was designated 'High Level' and the old station renamed 'Low Level'. The platform buildings were demolished *c.* 1971 but the chord line remained in use for a few years for freight traffic until at least 1973. The track was lifted by 1975 and the bridge over London Road was demolished in January 1978. The booking office found a number of new uses, first as the Nottingham Antiques Centre and then a restaurant when it became the Grand Central Diner.

Trams at Trent Bridge Junction (bottom of London Road and Trent Embankment) making the last journey on the Basford to Bulwell route in May 1934.

Nottingham Canal, 1925, looking west from Carrington Street. The Nottingham Canal originally proceeded from the Trent at Nottingham, Wollaton and Cossall to Langley Mill nearly 15 miles, where it joined the Cromford Canal. The act to build the canal was obtained in 1792, and the canal was completed in 1802. The man who designed and built the canal was William Jessop, who previously had success in designing and building the Cromford Canal.

Barges at the Trent Navigation Company wharf on the Nottingham Canal, 1908. With the Industrial Revolution came the birth of the railway, which overtook the canal as a viable economic transport route into Nottingham. As a result of the railway the canal quickly declined in use and became neglected. In recent years since the 1970s, the canal has enjoyed a 'rebirth' as a nature reserve and walking trail. The stretch of the canal in the city has especially enjoyed a new lease of life, with the area being well served by a number of pubs, restaurants, cafés, gyms and luxury apartments.

Lost Streets, Thoroughfares, Yards and Alleys

Drury Hill, Nottingham, *c.* 1906. Drury Hill was a picturesque and narrow thoroughfare. It was part of the old medieval business thoroughfare through Nottingham which came down Narrow Marsh and passed north along Bridlesmith Gate. Although very steep, the gradient of Drury Hill was comparatively slack when compared with the other medieval thoroughfares in Nottingham which included Long Stairs, Malin Hill and Hollow Stone. It must have been of very great importance, for when the town was fortified in Henry II's time, provision for a gateway, which Thoroton refers to as a postern, was made on the summit. The old name for Drury Hill was Vault Lane, which became Parkyn Lane, probably after some member of the Parkyn family of Bunny who lived there. It eventually changed to Drury Hill in around 1620.

Drury Hill, Nottingham, 1944. Drury Hill, with its narrowness and congestion, and its curious haphazard buildings, gives us some idea of the appearance of what medieval Nottingham would have looked like. It was eventually demolished in the 1960s.

Drury Hill, Nottingham, 1944, looking from the centre towards the Middle Pavement end of the road. This narrow lane was only 4 feet 10 inches wide at its narrowest point and signs had to be posted to alert traffic to this hazard. All of these buildings have now gone.

Drury Hill – Postern Place, Nottingham, *c.* 1969. North end of Drury Hill, looking south from Postern Place.

Middle Pavement, Nottingham, *c.* 1890s. Drury Hill is on the right-hand side. The Old Postern Gate public house can be seen in the photograph. This was demolished in the late 1920s.

Broadmarsh Shopping Centre demolition, 28 January 2020. The location of the photograph is taken approximately where Drury Hill once stood. The photograph shows the next stage of the site's history with the demolition and redevelopment of the Broadmarsh area.

Malt Mill Lane, Narrow Marsh, Nottingham. Malt Mill Lane ran between Cliff Road and Canal Street. The gate behind the lamp on the left led to Fitchett's timber yard and on the right is the Fergus O'Connor, a Shipstone's pub named after the fiery Irish-born politician who was elected MP for Nottingham in 1847. Also leading off Malt Mill Lane was Chapman's Yard and it was there, in 1905, that a young lad named Albert Matthews was murdered. His killer was John Hutchinson, who was lodging at Albert's house and was babysitting the five-year-old boy one night. Hutchinson, a heavy drinker, would later claim that Albert had thrown a heavy poker at him and, enraged by the boy's act, he hit him across the throat with the edge of his hand.

Malt Mill Lane, Narrow Marsh, *c.* 1920s. Nottingham was originally founded on a sandstone outcrop, below which to the south were flood meadows towards the River Trent. St. Mary's Church was established on the eastern end of this outcrop, and the Saxon town developed here. In the eleventh century the Normans built a castle on the western side. In the late eighteenth century the Beeston Canal was cut and this roughly followed the line of the River Leen from the River Trent towards Nottingham and below the town on the sandstone. The River Leen was yet again diverted. The areas of Broad Marsh and Narrow Marsh were therefore freed from flooding problems and they were built on. There was a thoroughfare named Narrow Marsh as well as the whole area being so called, and this was changed at one time to Red Lion Street, after the notorious public house.

Nottingham College construction, 20 September 2019. The area where Nottingham College stands covers the area where Malt Mill Lane once stood. Malt Mill Lane was one of the last streets to exist from the old Narrow Marsh. The college's location includes a purpose-built state-of-the-art 'City Hub' in Nottingham city centre. The City Hub offers new facilities and resources for students and provides community facilities such as a new training restaurant, café and performing arts centre. Building work started on the £58 million City Hub in May 2018. The City Hub project is part of the wider Broadmarsh regeneration plans led by Nottingham City Council.

Middle Marsh, Nottingham, *c.* 1900. Junction with Drury Hill (right). Middle Marsh and Drury Hill are no longer there; they were demolished to make way for the Broadmarsh Shopping Centre.

Long Stairs, Nottingham, 1913, looking down towards Narrow Marsh. The stairs were closed in 1933 and are gated at the top.

Red Lion Street, Narrow Marsh, Nottingham, *c.* 1919. This area was demolished in 1929. All the houses were replaced by some of the first purpose-built council houses in Nottingham. Narrow Marsh lay beneath the cliff on which stands the Lace Market. The area was notorious for its slum dwellings and outbreaks of cholera and other diseases. Note here the open drains and the woman getting water from a standpipe.

Red Lion Street, Narrow Marsh, Nottingham, *c.* 1931. Demolished area of the 'slum' dwellings. Red Lion Street later became Cliff Road.

Sheep Lane (now Market Street), Upper Parliament Street, 1865. Market Street started out as a narrow alley called Sheep Lane but due to its limited width quite a few accidents happened. Pedestrians going up meeting carts coming down caused people to be squashed against the sides – usually resulting in bloodstains on the floor and wall. This led to the locals referring to it as Blood Lane.

Sheep Lane (now Market Street), Nottingham, 1860. When it was widened for civic improvements in 1866, the aim of the gentry was to name it Theatre Street. This was because it led from the Market Square to the Theatre Royal. The market people had other ideas and the night before the official unveiling some of them unscrewed the sign and replaced it with one stating 'Market Street'. The following day was market day. The local gentry and the market people congregated at the bottom of the newly widened Sheep Lane for the opening ceremony. The mayor pulled on the cord to reveal the new sign and proclaimed the new roadway to be Market Street. Even though a portion of the assembled crowd – mostly the gentry – complained, the new name Market Street stuck.

Finkhill Street in the old Broadmarsh area, with St Nicholas' Church in the background. Like its neighbour Narrow Marsh, this was both a single street and also the name of an area – a jumble of narrow streets and cramped houses which first developed during the thirteenth and fourteenth centuries. The whole area was revamped during the 1960s and '70s to make way for the Broadmarsh Shopping Centre. Newsagents Frank's was one of the last shops in the district to be knocked down, in 1969.

Grove Street, off Newcastle Street, Broadmarsh, 1934. This street was demolished to make way for the Broadmarsh Shopping Centre and bus station.

Maid Marian Way, St Nicholas' Church, Nottingham, 1955, viewed from the former Chesterfield Street after the houses were demolished in the 1930s. On the left of the church was the narrow St Nicholas' Church Walk. The end of the flight of steps led down to Walnut Tree Lane.

Walnut Tree Lane, Nottingham, *c.* 1953. The sites of demolished houses on Walnut Tree Lane, showing St Nicholas' Church tower in the centre. The original church was razed to the ground by Colonel Hutchinson in the Civil War. The new church was built in 1671–82. The houses in Walnut Tree Lane and the surrounding area were demolished to make way for Maid Marian Way, which was built in the 1960s. In the distance can be seen the dome of the Council House, built in the Old Market Place in 1927–29 by Cecil T. Howitt.

Amberley Street looking east to what is now Maid Marian Way from Postern Street, July 1958, showing buses waiting at Mount Street bus station and the Newton Building.

Walnut Tree Lane, Nottingham, *c.* 1953, showing partially demolished terraced houses at the junction of Walnut Tree Lane and Chesterfield Street. The houses in Walnut Tree Lane and the surrounding area were demolished to make way for Maid Marian Way in the 1960s.

Aerial shot of the former Maid Marian Way kiosk *c.* 1970s, looking downhill towards Friar Lane on the left-hand side. The kiosk was left in place filled in with hardcore and reinforced steel placed over the top. The opening was concreted over and then tarmacked. Pedestrian crossings are now in its place.

Maid Marian Way subway kiosk, Nottingham, 1967. This area has since been filled in with concrete and tarmacked over and a pedestrian crossing is now in its place.

Charlotte Street, Nottingham, 1896. Charlotte Street was demolished to make room for the Grand Central railway station (otherwise known as Victoria station) which opened in May 1900.

Charlotte Street, Nottingham, 1895. Charlotte Street was demolished to make room for the Victoria station. The station's construction was on a grand scale. A 13-acre (53,000 m^2) site was acquired at a cost of £473,000 in the heart of Nottingham's city centre. Negotiations for the land acquisition had taken three years. The construction called for the demolition of whole streets of some 1,300 houses, twenty-four public houses, and St Stephen's Church, Bunker's Hill. Around 600,000 cubic yards (460,000 m^3) of sandstone was excavated from the site. The site measured around 650 yards (590 m) in length from north to south and had an average width of 110 yards (100 m), with a tunnel at each end for access.

Cross Street (later Huntingdon Street), Nottingham, *c.* 1920s. Nile Row later became Nile Sreet and still exists. Cherry Street on the right no longer exists.

Valentine Place, Broadmarsh, Nottingham, *c.* 1930, showing housing in the Broadmarsh area of the city. This area was demolished in the 1920s and '30s. The Broadmarsh Shopping Centre was later built on the site.

Narrow Marsh/Middle Marsh Junction, Nottingham, *c.* early 1900s. The whole area in this photograph is now all demolished.

Red Lion Street, Narrow Marsh, Nottingham, *c.* 1919. The whole Narrow Marsh area was replaced by some of the first purpose-built council houses in Nottingham. The old Narrow Marsh area was located beneath the cliff on which stands the Lace Market. The area was notorious for its 'slum' dwellings and outbreaks of cholera and other diseases.

Sussex Square, Narrow Marsh, Nottingham, 1934. This area contained many slum and tenement dwellings. Note the frame-knitter windows on the upper storey of the houses. The stocking-frame was a hand-operated machine around the size of a small loom or small upright piano and was used to knit stockings or hose. Other small articles of clothing like hats, gloves, scarves or mufflers from wool, silk and cotton were also made. The framework knitters worked at home. They either had a frame shop or workshop in the garden or a special room often on the top floor of the house. This room would have a special extra-wide window to let in the maximum light for the stockinger to work. All of these houses shown in the photograph have now been lost and demolished.

Memories, Characters and Tales

This is Charlie the chimp, and he used to be an attraction at Gordon Scott's shoe shop for over thirty years. For years the shop was inside the Broadmarsh Shopping Centre before relocating to Lister Gate. The shoe shop has since closed and now Charlie is enjoying his retirement at Brewhouse Yard Museum – currently in storage, safe and sound.

'Xylophone Man' Frank Robinson plaque, Lister Gate, Nottingham. Anyone who has ever walked along the busy shopping street of Lister Gate in Nottingham's city centre before 2005 would have heard the distinctly 'unmelodious' sound of a 'tinkling' xylophone. This assault to the ears was the 'music' of Frank Robinson, Nottingham's favourite busker. Frank was certainly no musician, even by his own admission. He was there to entertain and would simply 'bang out' random notes in an attempt to play a tune. Around Christmas time Frank's music would vaguely resemble popular carols. Frank was a very private man and until his death in 2005, few people knew his real name. However, the instrument he used was in fact a child's toy known as a metallophone. Frank Robinson died on 4 July 2004. On 10 November 2005, a memorial plaque was unveiled on the very spot where Xylophone Man sat. The plaque simply reads: 'He played his xylophone here for fifteen years, bringing a smile to the faces of the people of Nottingham.'

'Old General' in St Peter's churchyard, Nottingham, *c.* 1840. The Old General was perhaps Nottingham's most famous well-loved eccentric. Most people of today don't know who the real Old General was, but they have perhaps heard of the pub which was located in Hyson Green. The Old General (real name Benjamin Mayo) was born around 1779 in Nottingham and lived most of his life with his mother. The well-respected Nottingham historian Potter Briscoe described Ben's appearance in great detail: 'he was very round shouldered and his stature was no more than four feet high. His eyes were dark grey and his forward was very prominent. He wore his shirt unbuttoned revealing his copper-coloured chest. It was said that his legs was badly deformed so that his progress, which was generally a jog-trot, was very peculiar.' Many funny tales are told of the Old General and there are too many to list here. Ben spent the later years of his life as a great well-known local character in Nottingham. He was simple minded but well loved by everyone. When his mother died he was taken in by a Mr Hudson of St Peter's Poorhouse. When Mr Hudson left Nottingham, Ben went to St Mary's Workhouse. The Old General did not settle here. After a time he had a fall and died from his injuries. He was buried in the old St Peter's churchyard, Broad Marsh burial ground.

Contemporary artist's impression of William Saville. The name of Nottingham man William Saville is written large in the annals of criminology and social history. It holds against it the direct responsibility for the deaths of at least twenty-one individuals and the serious injury of many more. However, Saville was no mass murderer. His crime was the murder of his wife and three children. It was the circumstances of his public execution outside Nottingham's Shire Hall on the 8 August 1844 which led to the unforeseen deaths and mutilations of his other victims. It also led directly to the change in the local authority's policy towards public hangings and indirectly influenced attitudes regarding capital punishment.

Frank Edmund Earp's artist's impression of Kitty Hudson, the girl from Arnold with the addiction to pins. The strangest case in the long history of Nottingham's General Hospital is perhaps that of Katherine (Kitty) Hudson. Kitty was the ninth patient to be admitted to the newly opened hospital on 4 August 1783. Her case caused much excitement in the medical profession and perhaps a little disbelief. Kitty developed a habit of putting sharp objects in her mouth. For Kitty, what began as a habit soon became an addiction and in her own words, she could 'neither eat, drink, nor sleep' without pins or needles in her mouth. Kitty began to suffer a constant numbness in her arms and legs which the doctors could not explain. When she was finally admitted to hospital Kitty's right arm was inflamed and infected. On examination, the doctors discovered two needles under the skin a little above the wrist. These were quickly extracted using forceps. Further examination revealed more needles higher up the arm, which were also extracted. With the exception of two or three short brakes when she was sent home, Kitty was to spend nearly two years in hospital until finally discharged as cured. Over this time the records show that she underwent numerous operations to remove 'Great numbers of pins, needles and pieces of carious bone were extracted from her feet, legs, arms and other parts of her body and both breasts were removed with the knife.'

Plaque marking Bendigo's birthplace in Trinity Walk, Nottingham. William 'Bendigo' Thompson was born in 1811 in New Yard, now Trinity Walk, off Parliament Street. The area Bendigo was brought up in was no more than slum-like compared to modern social housing. Naturally, the slums were rife with pestilence and disease, and the life expectancy here was less than half the national average — a shocking twenty-two years. The town boundaries had not changed since they were erected nearly 800 years before, and the Industrial Revolution led to massive overcrowding. A town that probably housed around 1,000 people when built now squeezed in around 50,000. One government official even labelled Nottingham as the 'worst town in England'. The worst-affected areas were Narrow Marsh and the streets crowded between Long Row and Parliament Street, the people here said to be 'the poorest of all Queen Victoria's children'. William Abednego Thompson (11 October 1811–23 August 1880) went on to become an English bare-knuckle boxer who won the heavyweight championship of England from James Burke on 12 February 1839. He was inducted into the Ring Boxing Hall of Fame in 1955 and the International Boxing Hall of Fame in 1991.

Xylophone Man Frank Robinson, Lister Gate, Nottingham, 1990s.

Sally Anne Freeman, the newspaper seller, Old Market Square, 1981. This edition of the *Evening Post* concerns the capture of the Yorkshire Ripper, which dates the photograph to exactly 23 May 1981. The well-spoken newspaper seller pictured here was also a popular pavement artist towards the latter half of the decade. Sally's current whereabouts are unknown.

Tug Wilson, Old Market Square, Nottingham, 1982. Ex-Grenadier Guard PC Dennis 'Tug' Wilson, standing 7 feet 2.5 inches tall to the tip of his helmet, was a familiar sight in Nottingham until the early 1980s. Dennis was a pall bearer and part of the cortege party at the funeral of King George VI in 1952.

Tales of Robin Hood was from 1989 to 2009 an indoor visitor attraction and medieval banqueting centre based on the Nottinghamshire legend of Robin Hood. The centre was located on Maid Marian Way in Nottingham city centre, in the vicinity of Nottingham Castle, and brought an estimated £2 million in tourism revenue to the city each year. Visitors were taken on a chair-lift ride through a recreation of medieval Nottingham, with its sights, sounds and smells in addition to Robin Hood's hideout in medieval Sherwood Forest. Archery and brass rubbing were also on offer and a cinema show investigated the legend of Robin Hood. The centre's 'Great Hall' offered medieval banquets throughout the year. The attraction was forced to close in January 2009, after twenty years of business, due to difficulties with rent payments to its landlord, Tesco.

The Mushy Pea Stall in Victoria Centre market, Nottingham, 2017, one of Nottingham's oldest traditions. Ever since the start of the Covid-19 pandemic in early 2020 stallholder Claire Fisher struggled due to lack of footfall and contemplated quitting, but she carried on after receiving financial help from government grants. However, business remained slow and the rising cost of peas was the final nail in the coffin, leading to Claire calling it a day in 2022.

Jermy & Westerman's antiquarian bookshop on Mansfield Road was one Nottingham's oldest existing independent bookshops. It was owned by Geoff Blore since 1978.

From left to right: Richard Blore and Geoff Blore of Jermy & Westerman, 203 Mansfield Road, Nottingham, NG1 3FS. The bookshop closed in 2019.

William Abednego Thompson (11 October 1811–23 August 1880), also known Bendigo Thompson, was an English bare-knuckle boxer who won the heavyweight championship of England from James Burke on 12 February 1839. William 'Bendigo' Thompson was born in 1811 in New Yard, now Trinity Walk, off Parliament Street.

Nottingham Street Busker Alan Powe outside C&A *c.* 1986 (on the left). Alan still playing his banjo in Australia around 2008 (on the right).

Mogs Morgan, saxophonist, outside H&M *c.* 1990s.

The Nottingham Goose Fair

Goose Fair in the Old Market Square, early 1900s. The earliest reference to a fair in Nottingham refers to a St Mathew's Fair of 21 September. A charter to hold a Martinmas Fair – 11 November – was granted by Henry II to the Priory of Lenton in 1164. This ran for eight days and was extended to twelve days sometime in the thirteenth century. The charter forbade the holding of any other fair or market in the district during this time and so eclipsed all other fairs in Nottingham. Lenton Fair continued until the Dissolution in 1536 but is still mentioned in Harrisons Calendar of Fairs in 1587.

Goose Fair, Market Square, *c.* 1910. Nottingham's Goose Fair is first recorded by name in the borough records of 1541. Goose Fair became famous as a 'cheese fair' but it is the Michaelmas Goose which is remembered and marked in its name. Geese hatched in the spring were ready for the table by Michaelmas and it became customary – for those able to afford it – to celebrate with a meal of a well-fattened goose. It was also customary for tenants to present their landlords, in part-payment of rent, with a fine brace of geese.

Goose Fair, Market Place, Nottingham, *c.* 1914. Looking north-west from South Parade towards Long Row central and Griffin and Spalding store. The goose is perhaps dearer to the hearts of the good folk of Nottingham, young and old, as the symbol of the much-celebrated Goose Fair. The fair, – at least in name – has been held almost continuously for over 400 years, but its origins are believed to be much older and there has been a fair held in Nottingham since the early medieval period.

The Nottingham Goose Fair, Market Place, Nottingham, *c.* early 1900s. Local legend tells how there was once a fisherman on the River Trent who, after fishing for a while and catching a few carp and other fish, had his bate taken by a monster pike. For some time, man and fish struggled in that conflict enjoyed by anglers. Eventually, the great fish tired and the man began to reel it towards the shore. At that moment, as the fish began to emerge from the water, a wild goose flying overhead swooped down and seized the fish in its beak. The goose flew high into the air with its prize, but the pike still had the bated hook in its mouth and the man still held tight to his rod. Imagine the scene when the goose flew over the Market Square with pike, rod and man dangling from its beak! The burden was too much for the bird and it released its grip. Down tumbled the angler, rod and fish. The astonished crowd in the square rushed to the man's aid, only to find him standing unhurt, for he had landed safely on his feet. In celebration of this wonderful event it was decided to hold a fair on the very spot where the man had landed and it was to be known as the Goose Fair.

Goose Fair in the Market Square, 1908.

Goose Fair, Market Place, Nottingham, *c*. 1907. The Ferris wheel at the Goose Fair. The fair was originally held in Nottingham for eight days of October, reduced to five days in 1876. The Market Place was filled with stalls, fairground rides, attractions, jugglers and entertainers, and inhabitants of Nottingham, both rich and poor.

Helter skelter, Goose Fair, Old Market Square, Nottingham, *c.* 1925.

Goose Fair, Old Market Square, Nottingham, *c*. 1925.

Nottingham Goose Fair, Old Market Square, Nottingham, *c.* 1920s. The idea of the attraction was to give money, and the bird picked an envelope out of the drawer which would predict the future of the paying 'customer'.

The last Goose Fair in the Market Square, 1927. For centuries the fair was held in Nottingham's Old Market Square in the city centre until it was moved to the Forest Recreation Ground in 1928 due to space limitations and planned redevelopment of the market square.

The Goose Fair, Forest Recreation Ground, 1928. This was the first year the fair was held on the Forest Recreation Ground.

Nottingham Goose Fair, Forest Recreation Ground, 1938.

Nottingham Goose Fair, Forest Recreation Ground, 1950s.

Nottingham Goose Fair, Forest Recreation Ground. A fascinating view of the Goose Fair with the Nottingham skyline stretching away in the background, 1955.

Nottingham Goose Fair, Forest Recreation Ground, 1956.

Nottingham Goose Fair, Forest Recreation Ground, 1962.

Nottingham Goose Fair, Forest Recreation Ground, Thursday evening in October 1964.

Nottingham Goose Fair, Forest Recreation Ground, 1973.

Goose Fair boxing booth with owner Ron Taylor.

Nottingham Goose Fair, Forest Recreation Ground. McDonald's at Goose Fair in 1994.

Also available from Amberley Publishing

ISBN 978 1 4456 5243 6

Also available from Amberley Publishing

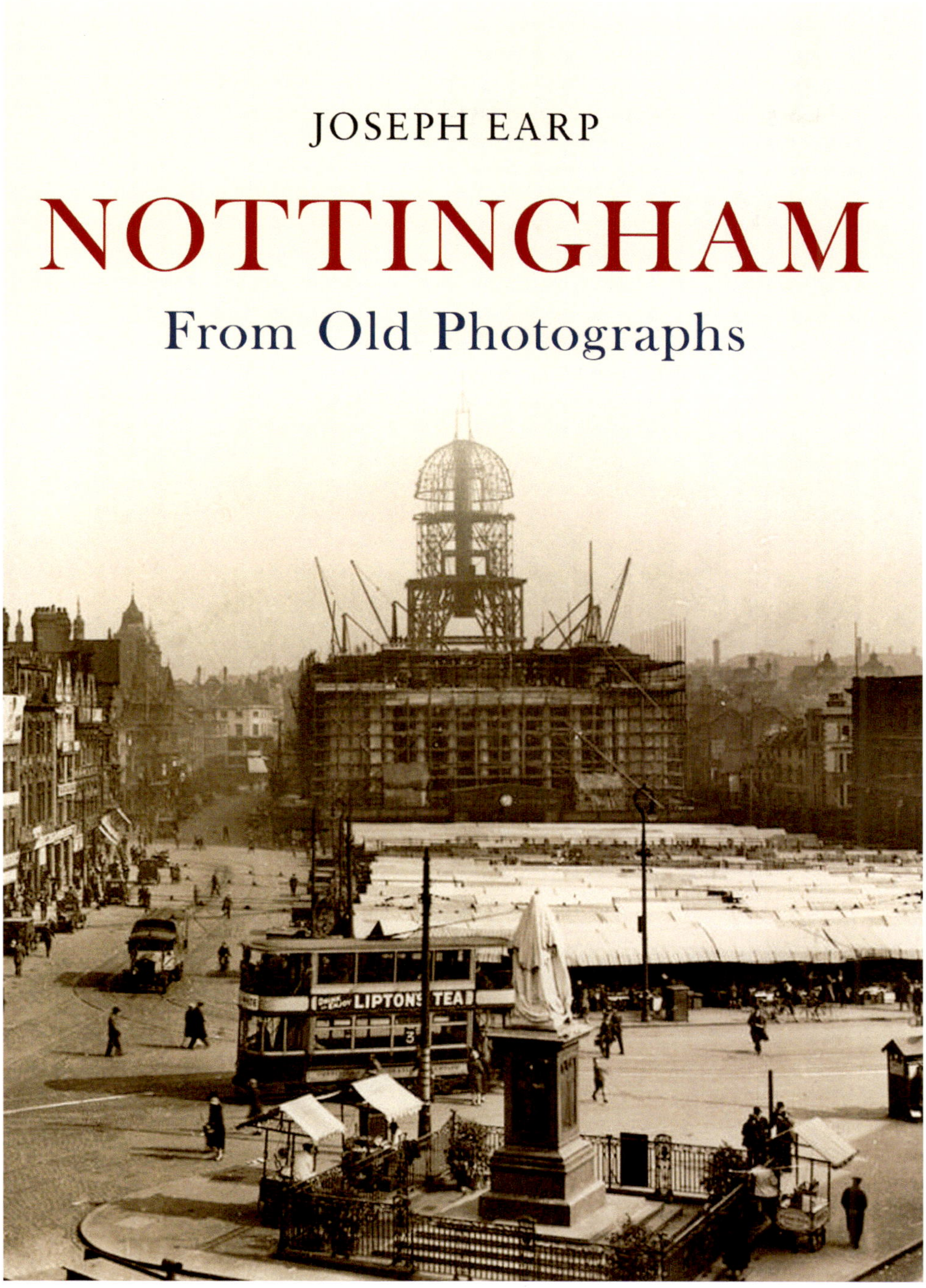

ISBN 978 1 4456 3459 3

Also available from Amberley Publishing

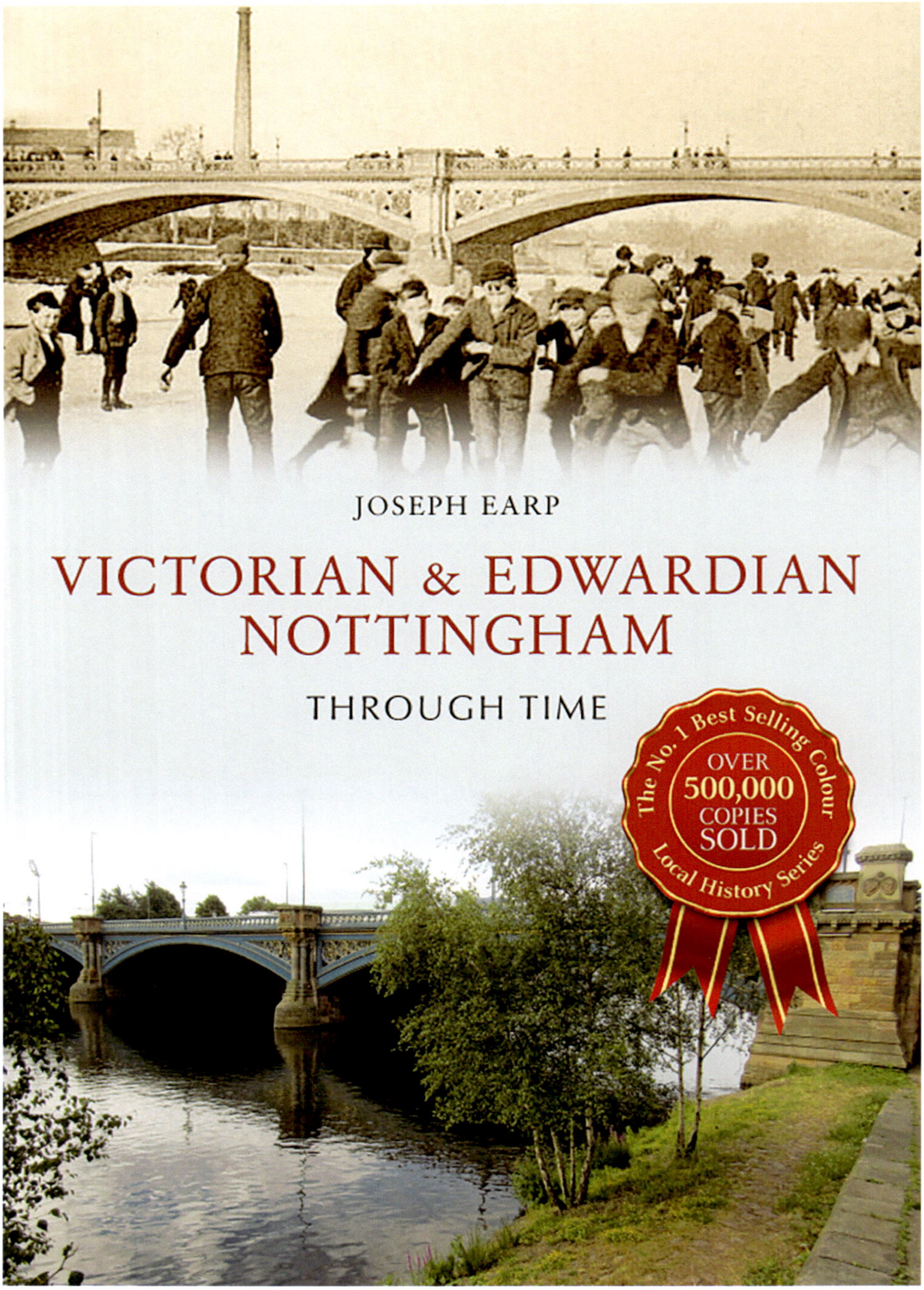

ISBN 978 1 4456 5656 4